Bride's Mound
Gateway to Avalon

Gordon Strong
Jane Marshall

Illustrated by
Jen Delyth

FLASHMAGIC7

First published in 2009 by FLASHMAGIC7

FLASHMAGIC7
BM Mutus Liber
London WC1N 3XX

A CIP catalogue record for this book is available from the British Library.

ISBN-13: 978-0955523045

www.mutusliber.com

Contents

Preface

I first met Jane Marshall at the Dion Fortune conference in Glastonbury in September 2007. Just after Samhain, I contacted her and suggested we write a book together about Bride's Mound. Not only in her role as secretary of the Friends of Bride's Mound has Jane served the Goddess, she has an unrivalled affinity and dedication to all that Bride represents. An exchange of letters followed, and it was obvious much of our thinking around Bride ran along the same lines. When all our material was collected together, we had a book that was the sum of both our views.

Through one of those marvellous occurrences of synchronicity that rule our lives, I met Jen Delyth, an artist, at the Stanton Drew stone circles. Later, when Jane and I were discussing illustrations for the book, I realised Jen would be the ideal candidate. Once more, marvellously, she agreed to be involved in the project.

In May 2008 my beloved Shama and I celebrated our Handfasting at Bride's Mound, providing an even deeper connection with this sacred place. By the end of this year the work was complete and with it Jane and I felt we had restored Bride's Mound to its proper place in the Isle of Avalon.

Gordon Strong
July 2009

Acknowledgements

I would like to thank Lone Bang for her contribution to the Astrology section, and also the poem that she gave us. Without Jen Delyth's beautiful illustrations the book would not be half so pleasing. I am grateful also to my son Ed for sorting out many of the technological details in the book's production. I must mention too my wonderful wife Shama, whose spirit is so bound up with Bride's Mound that I feel the Goddess has endlessly smiled upon our union.

Gordon Strong

I dedicate my writing to the Goddess, the Fellowship of Isis, and the 'holiest erthe' of Glastonbury in the Vale of Avalon. I also thank Gordon for giving me the opportunity to contribute to this book.

Jane Marshall

Bride Speaks:
Black the town yonder,
Black those that are in it,
I am the White swan,
Queen of them all.

Robert Graves

Glastonbury is not only deep rooted in the past, but the past lives on at Glastonbury. All about us it stirs and breathes, quiet but living and watching.

Dion Fortune

We need not believe that the Glastonbury legends are records of fact; but the existence of those legends is a very great fact.

E. A. Freeman

Earth and Water

The Somerset Levels are strange and atmospheric — a landscape of pollard willow, withy beds and low hills.

Patricia Wendorf

The geography of the county of Somerset is composed largely of moorland and isolated hills. The land adjoining the coast is below sea level, most of which regularly flooded until the beginning of the nineteenth century. At that time the draining of the Somerset levels began in earnest. The alluvial deposits, left after the land had dried out, made for rich pastures. The efforts of the Victorian engineers served to endow Somerset with a new image of abundance and fertility. Suddenly, an endless supply of cheese, strawberries and cider appeared to flow out of the West Country.

Ten thousand years ago, the water that came from the melting of the glaciers ensured that only a few points of land in low-lying Somerset were left visible. These 'islands' were Brean Down, Brent Knoll, Wedmore, Panborough, Godney, Meare, Glastonbury and Beckery. Travelling between these places was undertaken by boat, though the Neolithic peoples built wooden trackways across the marshland. The most celebrated of these is the *Sweet Track*, running a distance of one and a quarter miles from Westhay to Shapwick.

For a further five thousand years the Somerset Levels lay beneath the sea. Even two thousand years ago, most of the area now known as Somerset was still under water. From the Severn, later named the Bristol Channel, boats would pass by Brean Down, Cheddar and Loxton and eventually approach the West Glastonbury peninsula at Bride's Mound on the outskirts of Glastonbury. In Medieval times there may have been a harbour, below Wearyall Hill and Butleigh. No trace of this remains, and the less than dramatic rise of ground at Beckery is the feature that has been preserved in memory.

Bride's Mound is the key to the pattern of 'Ancient Hills' that give Glastonbury its physical character. From the mound, three leys radiate eastwards into the Isle of Avalon. The most northerly passes through the Magdalene Chapel to Gog and Magog, while beneath it another passes through the Chalice Well to the Tor. The third, southernmost line runs from Beckery to Wearyall Hill and from there to Cinnamon Lane. At the point where the 'middle' ley strikes Chalice Well it intersects with another ley passing from St. Edmunds Hill to Chalice Hill, thus all five points are energetically connected.

An Earth Energy line plotted by Tony Kennish,[1] and given the title 'Magdalen-St.Bridget', begins by following the aforementioned 'middle' ley reasonably faithfully. It then veers south at Fisher's Hill, skirts the edge of the Isle, hugs the road at Coursing Batch and completes its journey at Ponter's Ball. The exhaustive researches of Kennish, presently a native of Glastonbury, are particularly helpful to our study.

It can be readily seen that Bride's Mound was once as significant a location as Glastonbury Tor. It is no less than the Gateway to Avalon and a place of transition—one existing between two worlds. Timeless and indefinable, it reflects what it is—the domain of the Goddess.

---

[1] Anthony John Kennish, *The Glastonbury Chronicles*

Priestess

…what the slumbering Goddess knew would one day come through to her Priestess, and thence to the world of Men

Alan Richardson

The Feminine Principle is often misunderstood, even by some women. The Goddess has been depicted as mother, huntress, lover, virgin, artist, healer, destroyer and sorcerer. She embodies every aspect of woman—conscious and unconscious.

Figurines have been discovered dating from 30,000 years ago; they depict a mother goddess[2] of unknown origin. In the Hindu tradition, Tara (Sanskrit—*star*) is perhaps the most ancient female deity.[3] Later adopted by Buddhism, Tara became a most significant figure in the pantheon—the female Buddha. Having relinquished one goddess, the Hindu tradition produced Durga—a worthy replacement. She is exquisitely beautiful and very formidable, owning, among other gifts bestowed on her from her fellow deities, Rudra's trident and Indra's thunderbolt; her Celtic equivalent is Danu or Dana.

Eight thousand years ago the 'cradle of civilisation', the area around Sumeria, bore the goddess Siburi (later Sibyl or Cybele). Most celebrated among female deities is Hathor or Isis. She owns, among a myriad of titles, 'The Divine One', 'The Eye of Ra', 'Maker of the Sunrise', 'Lady of Life' and 'Lady of Love'.

Statues of female figures with the head of a bird or a serpent have also been discovered, both creatures having an affinity with

---

[2] A figurine from c. 3250 B.C. was found on the Somerset Levels.

[3] *The Stanzas of Dyzan* states that the 'eternal parent' is the Mother. Light, Chaos and Water are apparently the three elements of manifestation.

Bride. She has too, in common with *Neith* the Egyptian serpent goddess, the symbol of a *spindle* — to weave the web of life. The later title 'Bridget of the Mantle' may also refer to her weaving and spinning, or indeed the greening of the earth at Imbolc. The spiral, most dramatically present in the labyrinth that surrounds the Tor, is another of Bride's symbols.

The power that the moon exercises over water, demonstrated in the ebb and flow of the tides, would have been quickly realised by the ancients. At the same time the synchronicity of the menstrual cycle and the lunar month must have indicated the suitability of women as practioners of magic. The magical arts were as natural to our ancestors as breathing, there being in those times no artificial separation between the spiritual and the material worlds.

The Goddess unveils at each Full Moon, and her tri-partite character as the Virgin, Bride and Crone ensures she has mastery over each phase of our lives. Bligh-Bond, whose channelled scripts embrace much of Glastonbury lore, has this to say of the status of Brigit:

> She is virgin of old was Brigit and he bande. Let her
> goe to ye fielde yclept Bec Eyrie, in ye orcharde;
> there dreme...[4]

The term 'virgin' needs to be understood here. It originally meant 'a woman who belongs to no man', a fitting description of the Priestess who may be joined with the Priest in a union that may include sex, but one never profaned. The union of god and goddess, which every magical ritual endeavours to achieve, results in *total* understanding. The joining of the inner nature of the universe to the outer is known as *passing through the veil*. That veil is often thin in certain places on the physical plane at significant times of the year. Such a place is the Island of Avalon.

---

[4] Frederick Bligh-Bond, *Hill of Vision – A Forecast of the Great War and the Social Revolution with the Coming of the New Race* (1919)

Another, darker, view of the Goddess may be relevant to our study:

> ...the ninefold warrior hags, or her virgin form that of Angharad Goldenhand. She appears disguised as the Black Oppressor's daughter, or undisguised as the woman of the Mound. ...the Goddess appears as the Countess of the Games...[5]

Is the 'woman of the mound' an oblique reference to Bride's Mound? 'Undisguised' most certainly, for this is the Goddess in all her luminous splendour. Olivia Robertson describes her appearance from a vision, '...hair like liquid gold cut in "petals"... a white robe slightly flushed with gold..." [6]

The male shaman eventually became *the magician*, the female shaman — The Moon Priestess.[7] It was the latter who became guardian of the temple. As Dolores Ashcroft-Nowicki explains,

> A woman brings power into the temple, she is strongest on the Inner Levels and in deeper touch with the fluid world of the astral. A man is best at directing that power once it has been passed to him.[8]

It is said that on coastal areas the Moon Priestess became the 'Sea Priestess', a view comprehensively endorsed by Dion Fortune in her magical novel of the same name. Salt is the 'third heavenly substance' in alchemy, and represents the action of

---

[5] Malcolm Godwin, *The Holy Grail – Its Origins, Secrets & Meaning Revealed* (London: Bloomsbury, 1994), p. 62

[6] Olivia Robertson, *Nuit of the Milky Way* (London: F.O.I, 2007), p.7

[7] 'Daughter of the Moon', and as 'Keeper of the Sacred Flame', embraces both the light of the sun and the moon.

[8] Dolores Ashcroft-Nowicki, *The Ritual Magic Workbook – A Practical Course of Self-Initiation* (Wellingborough: The Aquarian Press, 1986) p.77

thought on matter. It is associated with the Ouroboros and the Astral Body. Significantly, it contains the nature of both sun and moon, indicating once more that the union of Priest and Priestess is essential for any manifestation to take place. As Dion Fortune explains,

> When the body of a woman is made an altar for the worship of the Goddess who is all beauty and magnetic life, and the man pours himself out in worship and sacrifice, keeping back no part of the price but giving his very self for love, seeing in his mate the priestess serving him in the worship—the goddess enters the temple, roses in her hands, and her doves flying around her, called down by the faith of her worshippers.[9]

The Lunar Realm is akin to the Inner Planes, the abode of magic. The Moon energy is a medium for solar and planetary energies, converted into a form that may be assimilated into the subconscious. Agrippa, writing of the moon in the fifteenth century, insisted that,

> ...her motion is to be observed before the others, as the parent of all conception... hence it is, that without the Moon intermediating, we cannot at any time attract the power of the superiors...[10]

The Earth is the living body of the Goddess. The Celts instinctively recognised that the female consciousness was not just the guardian of the kingdom; it was the very land itself. Perhaps they recalled a 'Golden Age', one that followed the nomadic era and became an agrarian age. Such a time, of husbandry and harvesting, was accompanied by a peaceful

---

[9] Dion Fortune, *The Sea Priestess* (New York: Samuel Weiser, 1999), p.25

[10] Cornelius Agrippa, *Three Books of Occult Philosophy* (St Paul, MN: Llewellyn Publications, 1997)

existence for all. Archaeologists can find no traces of weapons from this period, only agricultural implements. As Malcolm Godwin reveals,

> For while these mysterious peoples had all the technologies to fashion swords and shields they chose to make comic masks and fish-hooks instead.[11]

The Goddess embodies a respect and love for nature. The planet Earth is regarded as female (Gaiea), the very fabric of creation a manifestation of the Goddess. In Qabalistic terms, it is only through *Yesod* that we are able to perceive matter (*Malkuth*) at all. In ancient Egypt and Mesopotamia creation was regarded as a shared responsibility one of god *and* goddess. The possibility that *female* energy might be at the heart of creation would have been regarded as a very radical notion. This autonomous female power is personified in the *Dark Mother*—the supposed primal element of all existence. *Chaos* precedes form. Is the face of chaos female? It has generally been regarded as neutral. Yet Diarmid O'Murchu describes this state as 'a boiling, chaotic conundrum of raw potential'. Is this how we must regard the female psyche?

The Romans attempted to identify Bride with *Minerva*, or *Pallas Athene*. As Nicholas Mann explains,

> …another sanctuary of the ancient British goddess of fire, water, sexuality and sovereignty was at the hot spring to the north of Glastonbury at Bath. The Romans dedicated the spring to the goddess Sulis Minerva. Her name means the 'Solar Goddess of Wisdom', or more broadly 'the fire goddess in the waters of the earth.'[12]

---

[11] Godwin, p. 24.

[12] Nicholas Mann, *The Isle of Avalon - Sacred Mysteries of Arthur and Glastonbury*, (London: Green Magic, 1996) p.124

If Bride is to be associated with both Fire and Water, how are we to reconcile this apparent conflict? The solution lies in understanding the nature of the 'Dark Goddess', her 'Dark' and 'Light' being merely relative terms, to be seen as polarities, not opposites. The doctrine of duality embraced by Christianity produced the notion of 'good' and 'evil', and the story of Adam and Eve was interpreted as an indictment of female nature. The Church's later rejection and ultimate persecution of the Dark Goddess, in Lilith, resulted from an inability to respect and accommodate the feminine. Putting this kind of prejudice into a modern context, Marion Zimmer Bradley bemoans

> ...patriarchal attitudes, hatred of women, the pervasive and insidious attitude that mankind was made to dominate nature... the hypocrisy and cruelty of what passes for Christianity... let the Mother make it clear... that Spirit is One and that they are, in worshipping the goddess, worshipping the Divine...[13]

Many seem to be more comfortable with the term 'Wise Woman' or' Enchantress' rather than 'Crone' or 'Hag'. At the time of the gibbous moon, she presides over the gathering-in of crops and the guiding of souls into the Otherworld. As Demetra George wrote,

> She destroys in order to renew. The Dark Goddess is the mistress of transformation and She exists everywhere there is change.[14]

Zeus honoured Hecate, the goddess of the underworld above all others; he gave her dazzling gifts, a share of the earth and the

---

[13] Marion Zimmer Bradley, 'Thoughts on Avalon', The Literary Womens' Trust.

[14] Demetra George, *Mysteries of the Dark Moon* (San Francisco: Harper, 1992), p.228

barren sea. Given a place of honour in the starry sky and among the deathless gods, her rank is high. In that same tradition, the renowned *Lilith* must be a prime candidate for the first liberated woman. She is Adam's consort before Eve, and a woman who abandons 'man' because he tries to dominate her. The argument appears to be over preference in sexual positions. Lilith hotly protests, 'Why should I lie beneath you? I am your equal.' Right on, sister!

The 'Druidess College' at Beckery boasted Morgan le Fay as a pupil. Founded by Atlanteans, the establishment offered three separate degrees of instruction to the girls: 'Spinner', 'Wise Maiden' or 'Fay', respectively in the arts and crafts, herbalism and the magical arts. It is said that Morgan excelled in her calling but could not resist using those acquired skills for her own ends.

Morgan—the true love of Arthur, and one sought out and unconsciously worshipped by questing knights—is all seeing, and able to assume the appearance of the heart's desire of any man. Choosing to be a sorceress rather than a mighty warrior queen, she is the dark side of Mars—deadly if challenged. Richard Cavendish describes her as

> ...tall, commanding and seductively beautiful. Dominating, ruthless, sensual and unpredictable... sometimes benevolent... sometimes cruel... (with) formidable magical powers...

Although Dion Fortune is describing the way Isis has with her lovers, these strongly sexual sentiments could equally apply to Morgan le Fay: 'she awakeneth him with her kisses in the darkness' and 'he taketh life at her hands'.[15] The principle of transformation is inherent in the Goddess, primarily in the evoking of energy, 'Here is Kali, destroyer, for woman is the

---

[15] Dion Fortune, *Aspects of Occultism* (Wellingborough: The Aquarian Press, 1962)

destroyer that man may be borne again.'[16] As Moina Mathers, a member of the Golden Dawn, once explained,

> That is where the magical power of woman is found. She finds her force in her alliance with the sympathetic energies of Nature. And what is Nature if it is not an assemblage of thought clothed with matter and ideas which seek to materialize themselves?[17]

[16] Christine Hartley, *The Western Mystery Tradition – The Esoteric Heritage of the West* (Wellingborough: The Aquarian Press, 1968) p.43

[17] Moina Mathers (High Priestess Anari), 'Isis Worship in France' (Article, 1899)

Pagan Bride

*Her flower is the dandelion, of the bright gold of the sun; her bird is the
oyster catcher, and her gift is the cradle — for Bride presides over childbirth
and a birth in the spring is good luck for both mother and babe.*

Christine Hartley

Somerset was once known as the *Summerlands*. An annual emigration to the area took place every year. Those who settled around Glastonbury (Welsh — *glas* = green) probably made the district now know as Bovetown their home. We have little knowledge of how these Neolithic peoples lived, and of their beliefs, we can only speculate. Was there Goddess worship in Glastonbury similar to the Minoan culture on Crete in the millennium between 3000 and 2000 B.C.? It is said that the labyrinth on the Tor was constructed during that period, echoing the predilection of the Mediterranean culture for constructing spirals and mazes. If ritual magic was part of Neolithic customs, perhaps it was also practised at the site that became Bride's Mound. It seems likely that this place was made sacred in ancient times, and was a centre of Celtic Goddess worship.

Any meaningful discussion of 'Celtic' culture must begin with deciding who the 'Celts' (Greek — *Keltoi*) really were. The term is usually applied to the nomadic tribes that emerged from Europe in the period between 1000 B.C. and 500 B.C. Like most wandering peoples, they had no distinct pantheon of gods. Deities, legends and magical systems varied from tribe to tribe but an affinity with what might be termed the Great Spirit was generally recognised by all. The Celts recognised that the power of the universe was reflected in nature. The term *animism* is their view that everything was as one — creatures, humans, trees, rivers — all forming an interconnected whole.

The Celts certainly recognised a deity they named Bridhid, Brighide, Brigid (Fiery Arrow), Brighid, Bridie, Brig or Brigit — all the same goddess but with an endless variety of names. As this is a study of Bride, for reasons of clarity we have employed that form throughout the work. The name means 'one who exalts herself'. The word 'bridge' may derive from this source, giving us Bridport in Dorset and the Somerset town of Bridgwater. It is likely that 'brig' and 'brigantine' may derive from the root 'Brig', a reflection of the importance our island race once placed upon shipping. The Pictish tribe of *Brigantes* occupied territory in the south east of Ireland and later settled in the region of England that later became the Midlands. They affiliated themselves with Boudica, the queen of the Iceni tribe, who lived in what is now East Anglia. When the tribes openly revolted against Roman occupation, in 61 A.D., it was Boudica who led them. The queen was devoted to the war goddess Andraste or Andate, a fierce deity in the tradition of Victoria or Bellona. Bride has only one role that can be associated with war — as the goddess of smithcraft. Traditionally the smith was employed in making swords. It is more telling that Bride is the goddess of poetry and healing. She is the hidden heart of Albion. It is the imperious *Brigantia* who became the tutelary deity of the British Isles.

Brigid was the daughter of Dagda the Sun God, to whom the oak was sacred. She has the title 'Keeper of the Sacred Flame' and an actual flame, attended by nineteen silent virgins, was kept burning at Kildare in Ireland for a thousand years. It was finally extinguished by the Christians in their misplaced zeal to eradicate all things pagan. Brigid was also paired with *Anu* another Irish deity who, like Bride, is associated with cattle, the hearth and fertility.

Bride was born in the instant when night changed to day. She rose with the sun and a beam of flame was said to have sprung from her forehead.[18] It is this state of being on the

---

[18] Echoing the story of Athena, who is said to have sprung from the head of Zeus.

threshold of two worlds that firmly established Bride as a major deity among the Celts. They were fascinated by the point at which two different worlds meet: the shore, mountain peaks, and the change of seasons — portals between two places. Maintaining a cosmic balance is the essence of all magic, ancient or modern.

Of her mixed or adapted origins, Fiona MacLeod wrote,

> She may have been an ancestral Brighde, or that mysterious Anait whose Scythian name survives elsewhere in the Gaelic west, and nothing else of her ancient glory but that shadowy word. Perhaps, here the Celts remembered one whom they had heard of in Asian valleys or by the waters of the Nilus, and called upon Isis under a new name.[19]

Bride is by nature a domestic goddess, one of hearth and home, who presides at the birth of children. She is most certainly not a warrior goddess or even a 'creator goddess' - as is Arianrhod (*Silver Wheel*) - though Bride has some associations with the latter through the 'cauldron' myth. Arianrhod is herself the cauldron, its blackened base the night sky burned by the sun. Holes began to appear in the cauldron and made the stars, their light, the *Awen*. The link between the cauldron and the Grail we shall discuss later.

To fully comprehend the Celtic sensibility we must consider the male counterpart of Arianrhod. Cernunnos (Latin *cornu*, horn) is also known as 'Lord of the Animals' or the 'Horned God of the Hunt'. With a stag's antlers to show his potency (the stag is associated in Celtic lore with Fire and the South) festooned with many a torc, he is a shamanic figure. His ability to shape-shift is lyrically described in *The Song of Amergin*:

> I am a stag of seven tines,
> I am a wide flood on a plain,

---

[19] Mrs. William Sharp (arr.), *The Divine Adventure – The Works of "Fiona MacLeod", Vol. IV – Iona* (London: William Heinemann, 1925), p.171

I am a wind on the deep waters,
I am a shining tear of the sun,
I am a hawk on a cliff,
I am fair among flowers,
I am a god who sets the head afire with smoke.
I am a battle waging spear,
I am a salmon in the pool,
I am a hill of poetry,
I am a ruthless boar,
I am a threatening noise of the sea,
Who but I knows the secrets of the unhewn dolmen.

The wisdom of Cernunnos is symbolized by the ram-headed serpent which he holds, his intelligence by the rat, and his tenacity by the bear. This group of *chthonic* symbols indicates his familiarity with Death and the Otherworld. Cernunnos carries a purse of money, it being understood that treasure is always to be found in the underworld. Spiritual wealth too is also hidden and must be sought after by the hero upon his quest. Does this make Cernunnos also a guardian of the veil, a *god of initiation*? His role is intrinsic to the Celtic notion of the equality of male and female both in the mortal world and the beyond.

Cernunnos is the consort of Cerridwen, keeper of the Cauldron, and the Moon goddess. She is associated with death, regeneration and magical inspiration. The Horned God is born at the Winter Solstice,[20] marries the Goddess at Beltane, and dies at the Summer Solstice when the darkness returns. Cernunnos then alternates with his Moon Goddess in ruling over life and death. Thus the cycle of birth, death and reincarnation always continues. The union of god and goddess brings the greening of the harvest, and in the ancient myths, the creation of the World. The concept of a universe, the responsibility for which is shared

---

[20] Hence the correspondence with Capricorn the Goat, and the erroneous transformation of the goat, and Cernunnos, into the Christian Devil.

by both a male and female deity, can be traced to the Paleolithic era.

As a personification of nature, ruler of the woods and mountains, Cernunnos was portrayed by the Romans with three cranes flying above him. To them he was *Pan*, who later becomes the Green Man, ironically the subject of church carvings all over Europe. Before that he is Gwynn Ap Nudd (Welsh, *Heaven in the Mist*) ruler of Annwn. The thorn[21] is traditionally associated with fairies, as the elder is of witches and both trees are prolific in Somerset. The sound of bells is said to be a protection against wicked fairies. The Fairy Queen has bells on the harness of her steed to ward off evil, and perhaps Bridget's bell also served that purpose.

The Fairy kingdom harbours the roots of the World Tree and is the unconscious abode of unformed matter, elementals, wraiths and the demonic. Of the rest of the Tree, the trunk is the physical world, the branches, heaven. The symbolism relates to the origin of *Druid* — Wood= *wydd* = Derwydd.

It is said that Glastonbury was a Druid centre of learning and there may also have been a Druids' Grove on the present site of the Abbey ruins. Certainly the Christianized Saxons recorded finding a hybrid of Pagan and Christian ways in this part of Wessex. Bride is characterized both in Pagan and Christian lore as a maiden or virgin goddess, so she is hardly an appropriate mate for the Horned One. Cernunnos must be paired with a figure representing beauty and fertility, as the Greek goddess, Aphrodite. Any enactment of a union between god and goddess during a ritual at Bride's mound was likely to have been wanton and earthy.

Snowdrops, mistletoe and the lily are associated with Bride, and she has become synonymous with *Imbolc*, celebrated on the first day of February. This Celtic festival celebrates the Return of Life to the Land. In *Cailleach* (White Lady), another title Bride

---

[21] In Scotland a revered thorn tree prevented a road-widening scheme for seventy years!

has been given, we can see a link with *Gwenhwyfar,* or Guinevere as she is more popularly known. One of Arthur's three queens, her name means 'White Phantom', and she personifies the earthly soul of the kingdom.

Christian Bridget

That which is beyond even the concept of reality, that which transcends all thought. The myth puts you there all the time, gives you a line to connect with that mystery which you are.

Joseph Campbell

The granting of 'twelve hides of land' (1,440 acres) at Glastonbury to Joseph of Arimathea in 63 A.D. enabled him to build the first Christian church. The land, a gift of Arviragus of Silurai brother of Caractacus, is certainly mentioned in the Domesday Book. It was owned by the Abbey until the dissolution of the monasteries in the time of Henry VIII. It is significant that, while in Palestine, Christianity was forced into being a clandestine religion, in Britain it was openly proclaimed. It was not long before the 'Monastery of Perpetual Harmony', as Joseph named his Christian foundation, became a place of pilgrimage.

> It is pleasant to speculate that when early Christians arrived at the pagan sanctuary of Avalon they found a flourishing and ancient initiatory tradition based upon a doctrine of immortality, an entranceway to the Underworld and a cauldron of divine dispensation, sovereignty, healing and rebirth.[22]

The reality is somewhat different, though St. Bridget does absorb some of the pagan essence of Bride in her nature. Whether this is due solely to her Gaelic origins - on Iona she was known as Mary of the Gael - is debatable. Christianity in Ireland certainly remained autonomous for over a thousand years,

---

[22] Mann p. 22

coming under the authority of Rome much later than the Catholic Church in England. It could be that the 'Goddess energy' was well able to resist any attempt to modify it. A channelling in 1922 by Dion Fortune goes some way in accounting for this symbiosis of faiths:

> When the Church first came here it was a place of power and there was peace in the midst. The worship of the Sun passed into the worship of the Son... How could a small band of pilgrims, men of peace, not of war, have landed and built and dwelt, if those who held the island had not permitted and welcomed and given as a gift the land of which the church stood... For at heart both faiths are one... the unbroken tradition of Sacred Fire; there was not conquering, there was reception and the old faith carried on. And here you have a line of force that strikes its roots in the earth.[23]

Blissfully ignorant of such doctrinal matters, Bridget, the 'foster mother of Christ', was born at sunrise in 453 A.D. in County Louth, Ireland. A legendary tale of her as an infant being washed ashore on Iona from a coracle has all the hallmarks of the chosen child with no earthly parentage. Bridget is asked if she is of the Tuatha de Danaan, 'The peoples of Dana'[24] or the fairy folk. In response to the question, Bridget offers this song:

> I am but a little child,
> Dughall, son of Hugh, son of Art,
> But my garment shall be laid
> On the lord of the world,

---

[23] Gareth Knight, *Dion Fortune and the Inner Light* (Loughborough: Thoth Publications, 2000) pp. 73-74

[24] Anu shares aspects of Bride in her association with fertility and cattle, and the name is similar to the goddess Dana, but of proto-Indo origin.

Yea, surely it shall be that he
Shall lean against my bosom,
And I will give him peace,
And peace will I give to all who ask
Because of this mighty Prince,
And because of his Mother that is the daughter of
Peace.[25]

When later questioned by the Arch-Druid—of Iona, Bridget explains why she was so named by her father, also a druid in a vision he was told that his daughter must be named after a Great Goddess. The Arch-Druid then informs Bridget that she is there to fulfill an ancient prophecy.

Truly this child is an immortal… There shall be… a spotless maiden born of a virgin of the ancient immemorial race in Innisfail. And when for the seventh time the sacred year has come, she will hold Eternity in her lap as a white flower. Her maiden breast shall swell with milk for the prince of the World. She shall give suck to the King of the Elements.[26]

Bridget has to remain on Iona to 'learn of the sun and the wind', which she does before returning to Ireland. She is convinced of her spiritual destiny and is determined never to marry. Her father has other plans and arranges marriage to a local suitor, but Bridget refuses him. Soon after this incident she takes her vows, and later founds an abbey at Kildare known as *Cill-Dara*, the

----

[25] Mrs. William Sharp (arr.), *The Works of "Fiona MacLeod" Volume IV- Iona* (London: William Heinemann, 1925) p.174

[26] Ibid, p. 175

Church of the Oak.[27] The ancients worshipped these trees and many churches were built on the site of oaks. An edict from Pope Gregory, issued in the sixth century A.D, had ordered that pagan sites should be expunged of their heathen associations and transformed into places of Christian worship. To the north west of the island of Avalon two celebrated oaks, *Gog and Magog*, are all that remains of an avenue of trees that once led to the foot of Glastonbury Tor. They were perhaps once part of a Druid Grove.

St. Bridget later gave her name to convents all over Ireland. Her penchant for travelling led to her becoming the patron saint of sailors.[28] The saint inaugurated a monastery near the river Liffey within whose precincts there was a sacred bell. In an echo of Bride's role as a silversmith, she also became the patron saint of blacksmiths.

Gildas[29] and William of Malmesbury, both writing in the Early to High Middle Ages, tell of Bridget's visit to Britain in 488 A.D. The saint left behind her bell,[30] comb, weaving implements and mirror, all of which were later kept as relics in the Beckery Chapel. Visiting Irish pilgrims began a tradition of kissing these relics. Gildas also mentions 'The Monastery of the Holy Virgins', a foundation dedicated to Bridget's memory on Wearyall Hill, later known as the 'Women's Quarters'. Her image in the role of a milkmaid adorns the tower on the Tor next

---

[27]Giraldus Cambrensis, in *Topography of Ireland*, tells of a fine falcon that frequented the abbey, known as 'Bridget's Bird', supposedly a manifestation of Bridget about her duty of tending the scared flame.

[28] Also blacksmiths, infants, fugitives, poets, scholars and poultrymen.

[29] *De Excidis et Conquestu Brittanniae*

[30] It was lost at the Dissolution in 1538 and rediscovered in the twentieth century. The bell was then authenticated in bizarre circumstances, and became the property of Alice Buckton. Since her death, no trace of it has ever been found.

to Archangel Michael—Son of Light.[31] Bridget is known as the 'Bright One' and the sister of Michael.

St. Patrick, another celebrated Irish figure, was, according to Harry Jelley,[32] born near Banwell in Somerset. If this is so, another connection between the West Country and Christian Ireland has been established. It would appear that St. Patrick[33] was, like other Celtic saints, content to gently graft Christianity onto pagan ways. The ploy succeeded in the short term, as doctrinal edicts coming from as far away as Rome could be ignored.

In 670 A.D. land at Beckery (Beokeri)[34] and Martinsey was given to Glastonbury Abbey by King Cenwealh of the West Saxons. It was thought that the first occupant of the site may well have been a hermit from Nyland and subsequently buried beneath the altar of the chapel. A Benedictine community was established there by 971 A.D. and a chapel built. The building was then reconstructed in the tenth or eleventh century, stone replacing the original timber structure. By the thirteenth century the chapel had been improved to incorporate a slated roof. A 'priest's house' stood next to the chapel, one of several adjoining buildings that included a (no doubt well-appreciated) lavatorium.

Extensive archaeological investigations carried out in 1967-8 indicated the extent of the community. A ninth century cemetery

---

[31] Depicted with a set of scales. As Anubis weighs the heart of the deceased and judges it, so in the Christian Tradition does the Archangel Michael.

[32] Harry Jelley, *Saint Patrick's Somerset Birthplace* (Somerset: Cary Valley Historical Publications, 1998)

[33] March 17th provides another link between Somerset and Ireland: it is the feast day of Joseph of Arimathea, and also St. Patrick's Day.

[34] The etymology of 'Beckery' is confused. Becc-Eiru, is taken to be 'Little Ireland', the name persisting because of the association with Bride. It actually means 'bee-keeper's island'.

with sixty-three occupants was revealed. A stone-lined grave was also discovered, the skeleton within dating from the sixth century. It has been speculated that this was the disinterred bones of the aforementioned hermit of Nyland.

In 664 A.D., the Synod of Whitby gave York ecclesiastical precedence over Lindisfarne, and such conventions as the calculation of Easter Day were established. The Church was now established as a spiritual and secular authority. By the time of King Alfred, ecumenical Christianity had come to Britain in earnest, and the old ways retreated into the Celtic hinterlands. It might have been assumed that Glastonbury, having Joseph of Arimathea as its Christian founder, would be chosen as the location for a cathedral. Instead, that mantle was to pass to Wells. It was a move which was to instigate a violent rivalry between the two towns.

Glastonbury did of course have its Abbey, complete with mysterious links to the Tor in the form of underground tunnels between the two sites. The devotion to such things by the common people is recorded, and implies a continuing reverence to a pagan heritage. Over the coming centuries folk memories and customs would never entirely die out in Britain. Perhaps for this reason paganism remained and even flourished. This paradox is at the heart of what makes Glastonbury unique. John Cowper Powys speaks of

> ...the immemorial mystery of Glastonbury. Christians had one name for this Power, the ancient heathen inhabitants of this place had another, and quite a different one... Older than Christianity, older than the Druids, older than the gods of the Norsemen or Romans, older than the gods of Neolithic men...[35]

---

[35] John Cowper Powys, *A Glastonbury Romance* (London: The Bodley Head, 1933), p.1115

Two churches in Somerset are dedicated to St. Bridget, one at Brean[36] the other at Chelvey. Leys connecting these two sites and Bride's Mound are of interest for the number of ancient sites that they pass through.[37]

---

[36] The grandfather of the writer Gordon Strong, was Rev. E. A .H. Strong, the incumbent from 1920-1970, who took over the living from his father, the Rev. T. W. Strong.

[37] The ley from Beckery to Brean takes in the churches of Meare, Mark and East Brent; it also bisects the Glastonbury Lake Village. From Brean to Chelvey, Yatton church features as does a long barrow at Uphill and also the site of Locking Castle. The third side of the triangle features the churches of Brockley, Burrington and Rodney Stoke also passing through Aveline's Hole at Burrington and the henge at Gorsey Bigbury.

Pilgrim Way

All Christian roads lead to Britain.

Traditional Saying

Joseph of Arimathea was a successful dealer in metals in the first century A.D. Honoured with the Spanish title of *Noble Decurio*, meaning 'overseer' of a mining estate, Joseph owned a fleet of ships and made several voyages to Britain. His business would have involved trips to the silver and lead mines at Charterhouse in the Mendip Hills. In those times Axbridge, Loxton and Cheddar, now long-established Somerset towns, were all working ports. Mining had begun in the Iron Age and by 300 B.C. ore was being smelted and exported from Somerset, long before the Romans established any regular trading routes. The village of Priddy (*Pridd*—Welsh—'Earth') lies four miles to the south-east of Charterhouse and, besides being the site of St. Cuthbert's lead works, boasts one of the great legends of Somerset. It is said that the child Jesus visited Priddy, taken there by Joseph of Arimathea, his great-uncle and guardian.

Joseph established the first Christian church in Britain at Glastonbury in 63 A.D. He had founded a small cell before that date at Crewkerne, some twenty-five miles to the south west. Pilgrimage to Glastonbury increased rapidly in the first millennium, and by the end of the Middle Ages the 'George and Pilgrims' inn was catering for the influx of the Christian faithful.

The routes established by pilgrims often follow 'lines of force'. Those in the Isle of Avalon have been plotted in detail, most notably by Hamish Miller and Tony Kennish. The most significant of these is the *Michael Line* - a Ley - which can be traced across the country from Lands End to Hopton-on-sea in Norfolk. It is said that the infant Jesus walked part of the

Michael Line—from St. Michael's Mount in Cornwall to Glastonbury. Quite the most interesting feature on this route is the artificial mound known as Burrow Mump. Crowned with a ruined church, almost an echo of the Tor, its construction must have been prompted by a desire to formalize the pilgrim way.

The *Michael Energy Line*, however, follows a much different route, as does the *Mary* line.[38] These two snake across the landscape, occasionally intertwining. The Mary line has a particularly organic pattern, in keeping with the goddess energy that bestows its power. It is also possible to plot another significant energy line, one which takes in the Magdalene Chapel before skirting the Abbey grounds, passing briefly along Dod Lane, and ending at the ancient oaks of Gog and Magog.

Hermes is the guardian and guide of travellers; he stands at the meeting of ways and haunts dragon paths and leys. Once he had his own mark in every hamlet, later to be replaced by the market cross. The presence of a mercurial energy in Avalon is evident in the Will o' the Wisp or the King of the Fairies whose kingdom is inside the Tor. The progenitor of Hermes is Thoth, the indispensable ally to the gods, particularly in his aid to the great triumvirate of Isis and Osiris and their son Horus. Thoth is their teacher, particularly of Isis, and their scribe and healer. His association with lunar energy - he is depicted with a crescent moon above him - is pertinent. In Qabalistic terms the path that connects Hod (Mercury) and Yesod (the Moon) is ruled by the Tarot Sun. The significance is clear: the Magus instructs the Goddess in the *practice* of magic, who in return bestows the gift of feminine intuition upon him. Combined with the solar power of this path, Mercury personifies the *polarity of magic*. He knows that the interaction and eventual union of the male and female — their combined will – creates *magical power*. As with Pan and

---

[38] Confusion often exists between the terms 'ley lines', 'energy lines' and 'alignments'. The issue is not made any easier by the use of hybrid terms such as 'energy leys'. A general rule is that energy lines can only be plotted by dowsing in the field.

Aphrodite, and perhaps Arthur and Morgan le Fay, thus do male and female energies meet in the Sacred Isle.

The title 'Pilgrim's Way' was chosen by Alice Buckton, a celebrated Avalonian figure in the 1920s, for an annual procession from the Chalice Well to Beckery. Devotees of the Goddess still follow this route at Imbolc. The route takes in Fisher's Hill and Wearyall Hill, where Joseph chose to plant his staff, preferring that location to the Tor.

In John 19:25 it is reported that, at his death, Jesus was attended by the three Marys—his mother, aunt and Mary Magdalene. Arthur, too at his death is accompanied by three mourning queens, Guinevere, Morgan le Fay and Vivienne. The common Mithraic symbolism of the two figures is self-evident. Joseph of Arimathea in the company of other saints is said to have brought, in the company of other saints, Mary Magdalene to Britain. The chapel on Bride's Mound was originally hers but was rededicated to St. Bridget in 488 A.D. Mary Magdalene is the inheritor of the Gnostic notion of *The Holy Spirit*—symbolized by the Dove. 'Wisdom' also has the Dove as its symbol and is considered to be exclusively female. The thinking of woman embodies that rare quality—*common sense*—practical, personal and applied. The Gnostic Gospels stressed the need for Divine Union—that equality between male and female that creates harmony in the individual, and thus among society. Mary Magdalene represents Action and Word meeting with Wisdom. Jung, linking the unconscious to the feminine, describes what happens when the female element is not given equal consideration:

> As the distance… between the conscious and the unconscious increases… it frequently happens that the opposites contained in the Great Mother image split apart. We then get a good fairy and a wicked fairy, or a benevolent Goddess and one who is malevolent and dangerous. In Western antiquity… the opposites often remain united in the same figure,

though this paradox does not disturb the primitive mind in the least.[39]

When the later Christian Church made to remove any feminine influence from the Trinity, it became transmuted into Sophia or the Black Madonna. The Victorian writer C. W. King maintained that some Madonna effigies were actually basalt statues of Isis and bore the inscription, 'Immaculate is Our Lady Isis.'

Another name for Sophia is *Philosophia*. A woodcut entitled 'The Female' by Albrecht Dürer, has an inscription beneath the figure describing her as

> That which constitutes the essence of heaven, earth, air and water, and that which embraces the life of man, as well as that which the fiery God creates in the whole world: I, Philosophia, bear all in my breast.

The numbers five and seven seem pertinent to our study — Mary Magdalene was said to have been 'cleansed of seven demons'. Was this just an early form of chakra balancing? After the death of Osiris, Isis is said to have wandered with seven scorpions, perhaps a reference to the unfettered quality of the female psyche. Specifically associated with Mary Magdalene is the rose — five petalled, depicting perfection. The rose is a symbol of Venus — love, beauty, and the *understanding of how vital are those qualities to the world*. That notion is embodied in *Shekinah* (Hebrew, 'to settle' or 'reside') — the female manifestation of God in humanity. The Gnostic Gospel of Thomas declares,

> When you make the two one, and when you make the inner the outer and the outer as the inner and the above as the below, and when you make the male and female a single one, then shall you enter the kingdom.

---

[39] C. G. Jung, *The Archetypes and the Collective Unconscious* (1926) p. 102

Christianity, lacking a symbol to represent femininity in all its aspects, adopted the *Mystic Rose* as an epithet for the Virgin. Bligh-Bond, in *The Glastonbury Scripts*,[40] records a channelling by Mrs. Hester Travers-Smith of the bringing of the Blood of Christ, the Sangreal, to Glastonbury. The reference of this theme to Mary Magdalene within the channelled words is unmistakable. The Church was never entirely at ease with the elevation of the other Mary, the Virgin, to an equal status with Christ. Thus the ecclesiastical authorities set about condemning 'Mariolatry', as they liked to title the practice. In Britain this schism eventually culminated in the division of the Protestant and Catholic faith. In this unhappy period, fundamentalists destroyed many images of the Virgin in Catholic churches. The Church's other misogynist ploy was to besmirch the reputation of Mary Magdalene, condemning her as a whore. It is ironic that the modern thesis of Mary bearing Christ's child would have been a heresy beyond comprehension to the Medieval mind.

---

[40] F. Bligh-Bond, *The Glastonbury Scripts Nos. 6 & 8*, (London: The Scriptorium Publishing Association, 1924)

Wells and Fairies

Where a spring rises or water flows, there ought we to build altars and offer sacrifice.

Seneca

The element of Water is by nature flowing, weaving and free.

It reflects, and thus divines, the *complete meaning* of any action. Nothing is ever totally good or totally bad—happenings in the material world merely demonstrate the possibilities of our potential as humans. Water has moods—from cruel to calm, and so does the water in wells. One speaks of a well of loneliness, of silence, joy, youth and immortality. A 'Bridewell' was a jail or 'house of correction', that euphemism for punishment so beloved of our moralistic forebears. Perhaps the siting of these places was a bid to eradicate pagan influences and replace them with 'Christian' virtue.

Once, votive offerings, known as *clooties*, were tied to a tree near the well. As they rotted away, so the specified illness or misfortune passed also. The legacy of this tradition is the throwing of coins into a 'wishing well'. The healing power of wells and springs is later reflected in the Grail—the power of a nature deity has been reduced to human terms. The beneficial powers of a well only operate at certain times. It is more potent at Beltane and on Midsummer's Eve than at any other season in the year. With the coming of St Bridget it was said that healing wells would only be effective on her feast day[41] and that for only an hour after midnight.

---

[41] February 1st. Known as Imbolc to Druids and the first Quarter Day of the calendar year. The Druidic year begins at Samahain on Nov 1st.

Every well has a guardian spirit which might be a cat, bird or fish. If it has a human form it might be a hideous hag or a beautiful maiden. The well and the fish are both equally potent symbols of the Goddess. In Ireland, for a fish to live in a well was considered to be a good omen, it being regarded as the guardian spirit of the well. *Ichthyic*, 'pertaining to, or characteristic of fishes'[42] has its root in *Ichthys*, the son of the sea goddess *Atargatis*. The word also meant 'womb' in ancient Greek. The *Vesica Piscis*, adopted by Christianity as its own symbol might, when observed laterally, be a depiction of the goddess form.

As the fish is associated with visions and healing, wells have always been associated with regeneration and rebirth. In old German, 'well' and 'origin' are the same word. In another tradition, *Ishtar* is the ruler of springs; from there she raises the serpent energy. Traditionally wells are consecrated by the moon and protected by the Great Serpent which winds its coils about the entrance. The Bridie Cross, made at Imbolc from stalks of last year's corn, shares its symbolism with the serpent. Bride has an affinity with both fire and water. She is 'Keeper of the Flame' and 'Guardian of the Well'. Her role as Goddess of the Hearth and the New Moon also demonstrates this. It is a transformation, in the same way that the serpent sloughs its skin, supposedly around Imbolc. Manly P. Hall informs us that 'a serpent round an egg represents the movement of the Sun around the earth'[43] as does the Cross. A Gaelic hymn relates that

> Early on Bride's morning
> The serpent shall come from the hole;
> I will not molest the serpent
> Nor will the serpent molest me.

The serpent features strongly in cultures from the Aztec to the Aboriginal. Greece has the Minoan snake goddess and in China

---

[42] O. E. D.

[43] Manly P. Hall, *Secret Teaching of All Ages* (London: Penguin, 2003), p.273

serpent or dragon energy is a principle of Feng Shui. In Egyptian mythology the celebrated vision of Isis by Lucius Apuleius is particularly evocative:

> A boat-shaped dish of gold hung from her left hand and along the surface of the handle writhed an asp with a puffed throat and head raised ready to strike.[44]

The River Brue winding about The Brides, the fields surrounding the mound, appears to be particularly serpentine and Glastonbury Tor is sometimes referred to as the 'Dragon's Back' by those who climb it.

Wells abound in the isle of Avalon. The Chalice Well is the most celebrated, and least known is the well at The Tribunal. St. Edmund's Hill has a well, St. Joseph's Well is beneath the Mary Chapel in the Abbey and Paradise Well is to be found near the ancient oaks of Gog and Magog. Traditionally, Avalon owned seven springs, and in the eighteenth century, one Malcolm Challoner drank spring water at Chain Gate[45] in Magdalene Street. It effected a remarkable cure upon him and commercial exploitation of the 'healing waters' soon followed. Adam Stout, writing in the contemporary *Thorn and the Waters*, tells of 'Six mineral springs which issue from north side of St. Michael's Mount, commonly called Tor Hill'.[46] As a result Glastonbury briefly boasted a Pump Room at Chain Gate in 1755, although the enterprise was ultimately not the success Challoner may have imagined.

Bride's Mound is also known as *The Salmon of Beckery* and at the 'Salmon's Eye' was once a well, now concealed. The 'ancient

---

[44] Lucius Apuleius, *The Golden Ass*, Trans. P. G. Walsh (Oxford World's Classics, 1994)

[45] Challoner swore before a court that, 'Where this water descends from is Holy Ground, where a vast number of saints and martyrs have been buried'.

[46] Quoted in the *Bath Journal* April 1, 1751.

salmon of St. Bride' is formed in the landscape by 'The Ridge' which leads from Bride's Mound to the river Brue. In the 1920s Bride's Well was 'a shallow basin marked by an inscribed stone'.[47] This *Bridie Stone*, beside a hawthorn tree, is still a place for offerings. The original stone is now in a field owned by the Friends of Bride's Mound.

[47]Philip Rahtz and Lorna Watts, *Glastonbury: Myth and Archaeology* (Gloucestershire: Tempus, 2003), p.150

Arthur and Avalon

In war, he is the leader, foremost in personal prowess, and directing all military movements; in peace, he is the general protector of the injured and oppressed; he offers up moreover those public prayers and sacrifices which are intended to obtain for the whole people the favour of the gods.

Walter Bagehot

After the battle of Camlann, the dying Arthur makes his final journey. He is certain of his destination:

> To the island valley of Avilion:
> Where falls not hail, or rain or snow,
> Nor ever wind blows loudly; but it lies
> Deep-meadow'd, happy, fair with orchard-lawns
> And bowery hollows, crowned with sea
> Where I will heal me of my grievous wound.[48]

Geoffrey of Monmouth speaks of *Barinthus*, 'to whom the waters and the stars are well known', who navigated the barque that took the dying Arthur to Avalon. He is *Charon*, the ferryman of Greek myth who crosses the river Styx. As *St. Barrind* he follows St. Brendan on a journey to the 'Promised Land of Saints', a Christianised version of the Isle of the Blessed in the West — Avalon.

The Tuatha were driven to *Tir n'an Og* — 'Land of the Ever Young', and Morgan le Fay was one of their ilk. Avalon is now her abode and *Morgen*, as Malory prefers to name her, is one of

---

[48] Alfred Lord Tennyson, 'Morte D'Arthur', *English Poetry III; From Tennyson to Whitman* (Boston MA: Harvard Classics).

Nine sisters (who) rule by a pleasing set of laws those who come to them from our country. She who is first of them is more skilled in the healing arts and excels her sisters in the beauty of her person. Morgen is her name, and she has learned what useful properties all the herbs contain, so that she can cure sick bodies. She also knoes an art by which to change her shape and to cleave to the air on new wings like Daedalus; when she wishes she is at Brest, Chartres or Pavia and when she wills, she slips down from the air to your shores.[49]

Concerning Arthur's last journey, a Qabalistic correspondence is proposed by Margaret Lumley Brown:

The Water-Temple of Hod is connected with the Barge of Avalon in which Arthur is taken at death, and Morgan is the Psychopompos of this sphere, at a certain level of the Celtic Initiation system — to which King Arthur, Ogier the Dane, Thomas the Rhymer and others were withdrawn when summoned by its Queen.[50]

Morgan le Fay is the *bête noir* of the Christian in the Arthuriad because she displays the wayward, lustful aspect of the Goddess. Perhaps Isis provides the link between Morgan and Mary Magdalene. Does the anointing of Christ with spikenard oil not suggest some rite of the Priestess? It is significant that both Isis and the Virgin Mary have the title of the Queen of Heaven. Morgan le Fay is also associated with Fata Morgana the Queen of Faery who steals away mortal men to be her lovers. The

---

[49] Sir Thomas Malory, *Le Morte D'Arthur*, Ed. A.W. Pollard (London: Medici Society, 1929)

[50] Margaret Lumley Brown, *The Arthurian Formula*, Ed. Gareth Knight (Loughborough: Thoth Publications, 2006), p. 115

Forest of Broceliande in Brittany is the supposed location for her venery.

Avalon has many titles, *Emain Ablach*, The Isle of Women, The Fortress of Apples[51] and The Land of Promise. It is best regarded as a state of consciousness, as Dion Fortune explains,

> And there is a third way to Glastonbury, one of the secret, green roads of the soul—the Mystic Way that leads through the Hidden Door known only to the eye of vision. This is Avalon of the Heart to those who love her.[52]

A silver bough allows a mortal to enter and leave Avalon, a safeguard for those who do not wish to be permanently enslaved to enchantment.

Glastonbury Tor has such a commanding presence in the landscape it cannot help but dominate the inner world of Somerset. It resembles the primeval mound from whence the earth began—*Nun* in the Egyptian pantheon. To the visitor, it often evokes memories of the 'holiest erthe in the Temple of the Stars' or prompts associations that seem alien and yet familiar. Sir George Trevelyan explains that

> Holy mountains are veritable storehouses of spiritual power guarded by heavenly beings, a precious heritage... Those... on this plane are actually guardians of these Holy Places.[53]

---

[51] Bride is said to have owned an orchard of magical apples which kept all who ate them in a state of perpetual youth.

[52] Dion Fortune, *Avalon of the Heart* (Wellingborough: The Aquarian Press, 1978), p. 29

[53] Sir George Trevelyan, *A Vision of the Aquarian Age;* (London: Coventure Ltd, 1979)

Some writers are ambivalent about this supposed 'holiness'. Alan Richardson likens it to

> ...the breast of a vast and sleeping goddess, the tower on top being a nipple filled with milk. On good days the energies from the underworld spume into the atmosphere with the sense of a fountain; on others days it radiates an air of near menace.[54]

It is said that in 563 A.D. St. Columba ordered the destruction of a stone circle that crowned the Tor. His brief from the Pope was to 'purge all witches from the hill.' In 2002, Nancy and Charles Hollinrake of the Glastonbury Antiquarian Society announced that they had identified the foundations of this ancient temple on the Tor. Subsequent investigations[55] have proved to be even more interesting. Atasha McMillan speaks of the Tor as having

> ...a portion taken off the top, like a Greek temple but circular. Within it was the most beautiful mosaic type of floor, and was set out like a zodiac. There were twelve columns around it, whitish in colour. Under the flooring there was a hidden vault... the top was domed... trees and rushes and water all the way round.[56]

Taliesin, in the *Prophecy of Melkin*, spoke of the Isle of Avalon as 'hungry for the death of pagans'. As if to confirm his augury, in the twelfth century a church dedicated to St. Michael was built on the top of the Tor. Michael is the archangel associated with high places, and he fights the dragon to be found there, while his counterpart St. George dispatches these same creatures when

---

[54] Alan Richardson, *Priestess – The Life and Magic of Dion Fortune* (Loughborough: Thoth Publications, 2007), p. 241

[55] Alan Royce, 'A Temple on the Tor', *Avalon Magazine* 21, (2002) pp. 6-8

[56] Atasha McMillan, 'Magical Mystery Tor', *Avalon Magazine* 20 (2002)

they occupy the valleys below. Of the fate of the church, the earth spirits 'like wind which you cannot grasp and like water which you cannot grasp'[57] seemed to win the next round. An earthquake occurred at the end of the following century and left only the tower standing.

Pagan associations with the Tor are rife. The entrance to Annwn, the Celtic Underworld, is said to be here, referred to as being 'beyond the ninth wave'. It is said to be a portal, a 'crossover of inter-dimensional vibrational frequencies' or the Inner Planes so familiar to magicians. The Tor is whatever one wishes it to be, the only limit being the extent of the imagination. The seven terraces that wind around the Tor, easily visible from below, form a processional maze or labyrinth.[58]

Inside the Tor is the kingdom of Gwyn Ap Nudd, White Son of Night, Leader of the Wild Hunt and the King of the Fairies. He may be an incarnation of Merlin, as later Gwyn will be Puck and Morgan le Fay Titania. Gwyn's role is to lead departing souls to the goddess Cerridwen. Her stellar aspect is in Arianrhod, who presides over Caer Sidi, the place between the 'sunless sea and the shores of time' where souls await reincarnation. Dion Fortune warns of the nature of fairy folk:

> We may take them as being the elemental beings. They are quite different in kind from humanity. They have no Divine spark; they will be disintegrated at the end of this evolution and cease to exist, unless they can develop within themselves a spiritual nature.[59]

---

[57] Rev. E. J. Eitel, *Handbook of Chinese Buddhism* (Hong Kong, 1873)

[58] For an explanation of this phenomenon see Sig Lonegren, *Labyrinth: Ancient Myths and Modern Uses* (Glastonbury: Gothic Image, 1991), p. 6

[59] Dion Fortune, *Applied Magic and Aspects of Occultism* (London: HarperCollins, 1987), p. 47

Merlin's parentage was '…the son of a virgin nun and a fire spirit of a high order…'[60] His female counterpart Morgan le Fay was married to a Fairy King. 'Faery' is the prototype of humanity, the spirit before being given Promethean life. Of the two springs within the Tor, the Red Spring is 'human', the White Spring 'faery'.

The conversion of Arthur to Christianity is a well-documented episode. On Ash Wednesday in the Magdalene Chapel at Bride's Mound, the king encounters the Virgin Mary with the holy infant in her arms. She presents Arthur with a crystal cross, the image of which he incorporates into his new standard, discarding the original dragon.[61] By rejecting his pagan heritage did Arthur evoke the rage of Avalon? Certainly, from that moment, Morgan le Fay, the reputed Queen of Avalon, plots Arthur's downfall.

Arthur is a *Celtic* warrior king, a tradition divorced from that of the Romans, one that embraced warrior Queens as well as Kings. The Romans were never comfortable with this notion and gave Arthur the title of *Dux Bellorum* so as to make a distinction between him and any 'king' who might actually be a queen.

The myths surrounding a hero are as relevant as the biographical details of his 'real' life, because they are *eternal*. The qualities that he represents are part of the human psyche and none the less truthful for that. As Malcolm Godwin informs us,

> Heroes are free to annul their own personal histories and enter a timeless zone in which they actually become those great heroic archetypes.[62]

---

[60] Dion Fortune, *The Arthurian Formula* (Loughborough: Thoth Publications, 2006), p.43

[61] This design later became the arms of Glastonbury Abbey.

[62] Godwin, p. 132

What qualities are necessary for a charismatic leader to own? The followers of both Christ and King Arthur never question the authority of their Messiah. Terry Eagleton draws our attention to the foremost virtue shared by these two figures. 'The image of Jesus in the gospels is of someone who is fearless.'[63] Arthur, as does Christ, qualifies as a Mithraic figure:

> His personal ascendancy—derived from Divine countenance bestowed both upon himself individually and upon his race, and probably from accredited Divine descent—is the salient feature in the picture: the people hearken to his voice, embrace his propositions, and obey his orders...[64]

Of the same ilk is Osiris, who embodies the sacrificial priest. Dion Fortune has no doubts as to *his* impressive status:

> This priest-emperor, being a perfected soul of a previous evolution, is immeasurably superior to the rudimentary consciousness to whom he comes, for, having completed his evolution, he is of the plane of God, and intuition, recognizing this, invariably treats him as a divinity because Divinity is made manifest in him.[65]

These solar associations also echo *Kether*–'The Ancient of Days' at the zenith of the Qabalah Tree of Life. The crown and the halo are remarkably similar, and the derivation of the crown symbol reveals much. As Andrew Collins informs us,

---

[63] Terry Eagleton, *Observer* Review, *The Armchair Revolutionary*.

[64] Bagehot, p.84

[65] Dion Fortune, *The Training and Work of an Initiate* (London: The Aquarian Press, 1955), p. 84

In Persian myth it is portrayed as a semi-intelligent embodiment of divine power preserved within a ring of light the size of a crown, and passed on from one king to the next. Eventually it came to signify the golden sun-disc, usually shown with either seven or twelve rays, which over the millennia solidified into a golden circlet, or crown, traditionally worn by kings. The act of transferring the divine countenance, or crown, from one king to another, became known as the 'coronation', from the Latin *corona*, meaning 'crown'.[66]

All solar deities are healing deities, and all healing deities are solar, the exception being Thoth, the Egyptian god of magic and writing who became Mercury. As already stated, Bride may have originally been a sun-goddess, thus making a link with Arthur. It is also likely that St. Bridget and Arthur were contemporary with each other. In the constellations Arthur is linked to the Great Bear, also known as 'Arthur's Wain'. The seven-star constellation has always been considered significant and to this John Michell[67] links the seven island chapels of Avalon, namely at Avalon, Beckery, Godney, Martinsea, Meare, Panborough and Nyland.

Academics continue to argue over the exact geographical location of the Arthurian tales. The present writers simply seek to gather the threads of the tapestry which makes up Bride's Mound. Arthur plays a significant part in our study and we believe the setting for his endeavours to be the Isle of Avalon. Thus we conclude that Cadbury Camp, at nearby South Cadbury in Somerset, is Camelot. From there, in one of the early Arthurian tales, Guinevere is abducted from there by Melwas,

---

66 Andrew Collins, *Twenty-First Century Grail – The Quest for a Legend* (London: Virgin Books, 2004), p. 104

67 John Michell, *New Light on the Ancient Mystery of Glastonbury* (Glastonbury: Gothic Image Publications, 1997)

'King of the Summer Land' and taken to his fortress on Glastonbury Tor. The name Guinevere or *Gwythuyr* means 'White Shadow' or 'White Phantom'. Local people refer to the mists of Avalon as 'The White Lady of Sedgemoor' which may be a folk reference to Bride.

The way from Cadbury to the Tor is known as 'Arthur's Causeway'. At either the Midsummer or the Midwinter Solstice (both are mentioned in legend), Arthur may be seen riding out with his retinue. His horse is shod with silver shoes, and it is considered fortunate to glimpse a flash of these. Silver being the lunar metal, a tacit acknowledgment of the power of the Goddess may be intended.

Another tradition is that Cadbury is a hollow hill full of gold put there by the fairies that were forced to leave Olde England when bells were hung in churches. Fairies have an abhorrence of iron, and it is a said that only Puck was immune to the metal. It is worth noting that, until the Middle Ages when it was grudgingly accepted by the mercantile class, there was much resistance to silver coinage. It seems that true wealth was associated exclusively with gold, the metal of kings.

Like a vision of Heaven, a belief that good actually does triumph in the end, provides a fillip to our lives. As Lena and Jose Stevens tell us, 'Imagination connects us with the web of power and the spirit in all things'.[68] We are inspired by the tales of Arthur and, as all universal myths, they are rich and multi-layered.

---

[68] Jose & Lena S. Stevens, *Secrets of Shamanism* (New York: Avon Books, 2004), p.38

Lady of the Lake

As the goddess Brigit was the keeper of the wells it seems straightforward to suggest she is a candidate for the 'Lady of the Lake'.

Nicholas Mann

The Priestess has practised her magic in the Temple since ancient times. The wizard Merlin stands above others of his craft because he draws on the *anima* and the *animus* within his psyche. The most famous man of all those times,

> Merlin, who knew the range of all their arts,
> Had built the King his havens, ships and halls,
> Was also Bard, and he knew the starry heavens;
> The people called him wizard.[69]

His predecessors worked only with the will, but Merlin knew that the power of manifestation lies with the Goddess. The Qabalah illustrates this polarity in the path between *Chokmah* and *Binah* and, even more succinctly in that which connects *Netzach* and *Hod*. Merlin draws on the energy of the earth, but combines it with the other three elements. To him, Water is the Goddess of the Lake, the wind is purifying thought and Fire— lightning. His legacy is perhaps in the character of Woden, who

> …stalked the rolling down land, one-eyed and wise beyond all knowing in cloak and hood when the weather was fine, stopping at crossroads to recognise his own dangling from the gallows, but on black and

---

[69] Tennyson

stormy nights he racketed across the sky at the head of his wild hunt of lost and noisy souls.[70]

It may be the power of Merlin that manifests the Quest in the first place, for when he passes out of the tale the Quest is at an end. Merlin is the 'conscience' and the 'consciousness' of the Knights, as

> the function of thinking was performed for the others by Merlin, who by reason of his two-fold descent — his father was a devil, his mother a pure maiden—knew the secrets of both past and future and therefore to some extent possessed both Promethean and Epimethean thinking.[71]

Merlin's own demise is at the hands of the nymph Vivienne or Nimmue who beguiles him. Myths often echo previous myths, as when Isis obtained the secret name of *Ra* and thus the ultimate power of magic by nefarious means. Much is made of the foolishness of the old wizard but this is a shallow reading of the situation. It is more that Merlin is a seer and

> knowingly surrenders himself to Vivien's bewitchment, to enchantment through the arts of enticement, knowing what he is handling over to her bit by bit… he raise himself to the calm untroubled heights of an Indian god, who withdraws unconcerned from the world into the stillness of the Self.[72]

---

[70] www.englishheathenism.homestead.com

[71] Emma Jung and Marie–Louise von Franz, *The Grail Legend* (Princeton: Princeton University Press, 1998), p. 55.

[72] Jung, Franz, p.395

Merlin introduces Arthur to the Lady of the Lake from whom he receives the enchanted sword. One of the four treasures of the Tuatha da Danaan was the Singing Sword of Cu Chulainn. From this is derived 'Excalibur' (*Caladfwlch* or *Calad-bolg* — 'hard lightning'). The ancients told that 'Fire springs from the serpents upon the hilt' and Malory, describing Arthur wielding Excalibur in battle, insists that it was 'made in the Isle of Avalon... so bright in his enemies eyes it gave light like thirty torches'.[73] Merlin reveals its hidden nature in this exchange with Arthur:

'Like ye better the sword or the scabbard?'

'I like better the sword', said Arthur.

'Ye are the more unwise, for the scabbard is worth ten of the sword; for while ye keep the scabbard upon you ye shall lose no blood, be ye ever so sore wounded.'

Is this a suggestion that Excalibur should be constantly sheathed, perhaps in permanent union with the Goddess? The sexual overtones cannot be overlooked, for the king must give his seed to the kingdom that it continues to be fertile. In ancient ritual the king would be physically united with the Priestess in her role as the Goddess of the Earth. Perhaps Arthur must be united with Brigante, the spirit of Britain. Bride possesses her own formidable weapon, the Sword of Light, so perhaps she and Arthur are united in the polarity between the Sun and Moon.

The actual lake that is the abode of the Lady could be Meare Pool, or the Waters of Avalon at Pomparles Bridge. This crossing of the river Brue by Bride's Mound is between Cradlebridge (Bridie's Bed) and Cowbridge, both having symbols linked to Bride. The bridge was supposedly constructed by descendants of the Well Maidens at the same time as the Castle of Maidens and Orgellus Castle. *Pons Perilis*, as it also known, is an allegory of the strict discipline needed by the questing knight, 'a way as

---

[73] Malory

narrow as the blade of a sword and narrow as its edge.'[74] Before entering the Grail Castle, he must cross the *Bridge Perilous*, and he will have spent the previous night in prayer at the chapel on Bride's Mound. His armour is the lower self and his spurs the higher self and the bridge a psychic gateway where enlightenment can only be attained by discarding all previous notions of reality. As Gareth Knight explains,

> ...it was not the dangers of a river crossing that made this spot feared, but the spiritual terrors that here beset the questing soul on the final stage of the Quest journey. Here the Knights of the Graal watched all night until early the next morning when they might pass to the holy earth of Avalon, to be greeted by the Fisher King and shown the Graal with its guard of virgins within Chalice Hill. And some died of bliss at the sight, and none ever walked with men the same again.[75]

A fascinating dream that came to his native servant in Shanghai, and subsequently reported to Aleister Crowley, seems to indicate that Arthurian symbolism is not exclusive to the West.

> I was on the shore of a small lake. It was a wild country and the lake was surrounded by tall reeds, some of them growing in the water. The full moon was high in the sky, but there were clouds and mist. You were standing in front of me, sahib; quite motionless, lost in thought, as you always are, but you seemed to be waiting for someone. Now there was a rustling in the reeds, and out of them came a boat rowed by two beautiful women with long fair

---

[74] Fortune, p. 154

[75] Gareth Knight, Address at Leaping Hare Annual Conference (April 1st 2006)

hair, and front of the boat stood another woman, taller and fairer even than her sisters. The boat came slowly across to you; and then I saw that the woman held in her hands a great sword, long and straight, with a straight crosshilt which was heavy with rubies, emeralds and sapphires. She put this sword into your hands and you took it, but nothing was said.[76]

When Excalibur is returned to the lady of the lake, Arthur's reign is over. His guardianship of the kingdom ceases too. Is it any coincidence that with the death of Arthur the Christian era begins to take hold in England? The Goddess considers that it will be prudent to seek refuge. Where? It is to the Well, or even to the waters beneath the Tor. If the latter, this may account for her overwhelming presence that many feel in that sacred place.

[76] Aleister Crowley, *The Confessions - An Autohagiography* (London: Arkana, 1989)

Pisces and Aquarius

In the ancient world there were certain people who knew how to work with the physical world in order to create access to the spiritual.

Paul Devereux

In the 1920s a group who were later known as the 'Avalonians' gathered in Glastonbury. Among them were Alice Buckton, Frederick Bligh-Bond, Dr. Goodchild, Fiona Macleod, Rutland Broughton, Wellesley Tudor-Pole, Dion Fortune and John Cowper Powys. One of their associates, Katharine Maltwood, 'discovered' in 1925 that natural features of the landscape, in a thirty-mile radius around Glastonbury, were shapes conforming to the zodiacal figures. There were those who had always believed that a terrestrial zodiac existed somewhere in Britain. Some said it was a manifestation of the pattern of zodiac signs that formed part of a mosaic on the floor of the Lady Chapel in the Abbey. Maltwood, a British visionary in the tradition of William Blake,[77] was convinced that the Glastonbury Zodiac was more ancient, older even than Solomon's Temple. She believed that a visiting race, the Sumer-Chaldeans, had 'planted' this zodiac on the land in 2700 B.C.[78] In 1935 Maltwood

---

[77] Blake wrote,

Heaven Above, Heaven Beneath,
Stars Above, Stars Beneath,
All that is above, is also beneath.

[78] Madame Blavatsky favoured the idea of a construction by Egyptian initiates. These were said to be trained at the Temple of Hathor in Denderah specifically to build 'colossal Zodiacs' in the British Isles.

anonymously published her findings in *A Guide to Glastonbury's Temple of the Stars*. At the time, her work was not received well by the archeological establishment. It was not until her findings reached an enthusiastic American public in the 1960s that she achieved any recognition for her efforts.

Olive Pixley, a noted psychometrist of the 1930s, recalled a dawn gathering at the Tor when she observed

> an etheric serpent-like trail of energy, that became brighter as more people advanced to the top. Then the sun rose, and the raised serpent fused with light from the sun through the circle on the summit and the resultant energy shot out through the 'alignments' over the land.[79]

References to a terrestrial zodiac occur throughout English history. Taliesin, the bard and minstrel, once sang,

> I have been a toilsome chair above the Zodiac... My original country... was the region of the summer stars.

On the twelfth century *Tabula Smaragdina* was written,

> Heaven above, Heaven Below;
> Stars above, Stars below;
> All that is over, under shall show.
> Happy thou who the riddle readest.[80]

What is the purpose of reading the riddle? Is it to use the powers of the stars in the way that the magician follows the adage 'as above, so below.' Perhaps, as Alan Royce tells us, it is

---

[79] Nicholas R. Mann, *The Isle of Avalon - Sacred Mysteries of Arthur and Glastonbury* (Glastonbury: Green Magic, 2001), p. 64

[80] Dimitri Merejkowski, *The Forerunner-The Romance of Leonardo da Vinci* (London: Constable and Company, 1933)

to draw down either moon or stars, thus distilling starlight from various parts of the constellations to attune with parts of the body that link with the zodiac and the 'Serpentsoul' within the body.[81]

The writings of the Elizabethan occultist John Dee may further enlighten us. In 1574 he wrote,

> ...the starres which agree with their reproductions on the ground do lye onlie on the celestial path of the Sonne, moon and planets with the noble exception of Orion and Hercules... all the greater stares of Sagittarius fall on the hinde quarters of the horse... thus is astrologie and astronomie carefullie and exactly married and measured in a scientific reconstruction of the heavens which shews that the ancients understode all which today the lerned know to be facts.

His contemporary Nostradamus mentions 'the land of the great heavenly Temple', later realised to be a reference to Somerset. In the nineteenth century Madame Blavatsky, in a discussion of 'sidereal phenomena', refers to

> the plan of the Zodiac in the Upper Ocean or the heavens, a certain realm on Earth, and inland sea was concentrated and called 'the Abyss of learning.[82]

The area of Bride's Mound is included in the Piscean complex that is part of the Glastonbury Zodiac. The 'Salmon of Wisdom', the Celtic symbol already mentioned, is to be detected upon

---

[81] Alan Royce, 'The Serpent in the Bowl', *Avalon Magazine*, Spring 2008, (pp. 12-15)

[82] Madame Blavatsky, *The Secret Doctrine* (London: Theosophical Society, 1888)

Wearyall Hill. The creature is in the landscape, huge and stretching from the banks if the river Brue across Bride's Mound and onto Wirrall Park. A second feature, making the dual Piscean symbol, lies in nearby Street. When the constellation of Pisces is to be seen over the town, three stars within it appear to reflect terrestrial locations: one is over Abbey Grange, another in Street churchyard (originally Lantokay) and the third over Press Moor. A ley line apparently runs from this point all the way to Clonegal Castle in Carlow, Ireland. Here is to be found the Foundation centre of the Fellowship of Isis and within their temple is the Holy Well of Bridget. If Bride is a great healer and figure of service she will be aligned with the Pisces/Virgo axis. Given that the advent of the *Piscean Age* comes with the birth of Christ, St. Bridget might be seen as a Piscean archetype. She is the founder of several Christian communities and gives her name to the Brigidine Sisters, a religious order.

Our perspective changes radically if we begin to consider Bride as part of the Aquarian age. Aquarius is 'The Water Carrier' bringing the waters of healing and compassion to all humanity. The character of this fixed air sign is depicted succinctly in the Tarot card of The Star. The naked female figure represents an independent, radical view of the world. She is humanity as the 'Crown of Creation'—the visionary and pioneer. Perhaps Bride's Well, and the many springs throughout Britain dedicated to her, flow with the sacred waters of inspiration. We might recall that Bridget dramatically demonstrated her single-mindedness by refusing to embrace what she considered to be the stifling conventions of married life. She preferred instead to pursue her vision of founding an abbey in Ireland.

Aquarius is also the revolutionary, the catalyst that brings reform to society and a lightning change to the individual. Uranus, its planetary ruler, has brought new beliefs to challenge old faiths—The New Age is at hand. This eccentric and unpredictable planet has a correspondence with *The Fool* of the

Tarot. The spirit of alchemy is within this card—combining and refining parts of existence to create a new whole.

The solar element in the Aquarius/Leo axis gives Bride stability. The fire of Leo is reflected in the Phoenix which is the form in the landscape that represents the eleventh sign of the Glastonbury Zodiac. In the spirit of Aquarius, Bride is still an enigmatic figure, appearing at that point in history where old and new beliefs met. As we have discovered, Bride is associated with the elements of both fire and water. Is it too fanciful to suggest that together they create a mist that covers the landscape and shrouds her in mystery?

The first of February is the feast day of St. Bridget. Whether this date commemorates her birth or death is uncertain. It is also the first day of Spring in Ireland—'The return of the Flaming Wheel'. *Imbolc*, the Celtic quarter day, is also celebrated on this date. It was not always so, the time of the Imbolc celebration being determined by the day of the New Moon that fell nearest to the fifth of February. This date was considered significant to the ancients as it marked the halfway point between the Winter Solstice and the Spring Equinox. Whichever system we apply, the sun is still passing through the constellation of Aquarius when we celebrate Bride.

It would appear we have enough evidence to assign Aquarius to her and, if she was born at dawn as is suggested, then Bride would have Aquarius in the ascendant. If the moon was also in the same sign at the time of her birth, she would be a triple Aquarius! Like Tara the female Buddha, Bride has different colours assigned to her depending upon her role. Her act of adopting of black in Winter, white in Spring and red in Summer affirms the chameleon-like aspect of Aquarius.

Avalon has seven hills, seven springs and seven chapels and is tuned to a seven star constellation, the *Corona Borealis*. It is both the Round Table and the Cauldron. It belongs to *Bootes*, 'the keeper of the bears'. Arthur it may be recalled is associated with the bear. The moon goddess Arianrhod has 'the Castle of the Silver Circle' in that constellation.

Of the manner in which the signs of the zodiac are depicted in the landscape, three do not adhere to the conventional symbolism. Cancer is a ship, Libra, a dove and Aquarius a phoenix, as already noted. The phoenix, a symbol of resurrection and the solar principle is naturally aligned with Arthur. In the Glastonbury zodiac it covers an area that included St. Edmunds Hill, Chalice Hill and the Tor.

Additional figures such as Christ, the 'Girt Dog of Langport' and the Swan are all incorporated into the whole. The 'Dog' guards the entrance to the Temple of the Stars, as Cerberus is guardian of the Greek underworld, and Anubis fulfills the same role in the Egyptian tradition. Bridget owns the swan as one of her totems. Our ancestors were fascinated by that formation of stars known as the Northern Cross. They preferred to see a 'goose' and later as *Cygnus* — the swan.[83] This constellation is seen at its best in the Northern Hemisphere around the Summer Solstice. The swan in the Glastonbury landscape[84] perhaps refers to its rider *Cailleach*, the crone who rules the Winter months. As late as the Victorian era in Scotland, offerings of eggs and swan down were made to Bride/Bridget.

A symbol of the soul, this magnificent creature was revered by the Celts and employed in divination. The swan is associated with both the Sun and Mercury. The notion that a swan flies in the air, swims in water and nests upon the earth makes it a metaphor for shapeshifting. In Celtic mythology the children of the sea god Lir were transformed into swans. Mercury, as Thoth, journeys between this plane and the underworld and likewise Bridget attends the soul at both birth and death.

---

[83] See Andrew Collins, *The Cygnus Mystery* (London: Watkins, 2006)

[84] Ibid.

Grail, Bowl and Cauldron

When your lips touch the bowl that some call the grail and some the cauldron, the goddess will Herself impart to you the riddle of the Secret of life.

Colonel C. R. F. Seymour

It is not the purpose of this work to offer a history of The Grail, more to describe its associations with Bride. That said, some understanding of the way in which the Grail has been regarded since its inception is essential.

It seems certain that the idea of a supernatural vessel originated in Ireland and was one of the four great treasures. These were the Spear of Lugh, the Sword of Nuadu, the Stone of Fal and the Cauldron of the Dagda. The quaternity, or four-foldness, is a universal symbol, probably originating from the importance of the four cardinal directions to the ancients. W. B. Yeats, working with his first muse Maude Gonne, revealed that

> Maud learned in a trance, induced by staring at a talisman devised by Willie, that the initiation of the cauldron or cup is a purification, that of the stone power, that of the sword knowledge and subtlety, and that of the wands a supernatural inspiration. For Maud and Willie these were the four suits of the Tarot, as well as the four treasures of the Tuatha de Danaan.[85]

This 'Cauldron of Inspiration' was given to Dagda, the father of Bride. These treasures later became the *Four Hallows* of the Grail

---

[85] Monk Gibbon, *The Masterpiece and the Man – Yeats as I Knew Him* (London: Rupert Hart-Davis, 1959), p. 320

Quest. For the Celts the 'cauldron' was the embodiment of the Goddess, bountiful, all seeing. It was warmed by nine maidens[86] who bestowed the breath of Awen upon it. A Welsh bard describes the Awen as

> A river while it flows,
> I know its extent;
> I know when it disappears;
> I know when it fills;
> I know when it overflows;
> I know when it shrinks;
> I know what base
> There is beneath the sea.

It seems that the cauldron may have an even earlier incarnation. Dion Fortune speaks of an Atlantean connection:

> In Atlantis the Cup or Bowl was the Moon-Bowl (of the old Moon and the earliest stages of mankind) in which was a substance in actual contact with the Supernal.[87]

The most celebrated pagan artefact is the *Gundestrop Cauldron*. Discovered in 1891 in a bog in Denmark, it was constructed between the first and second century B.C. It may have been filled with wine, mead or even blood and probably used for scrying. Perhaps its purpose was to reflect the power of the heavens, as a witch 'draws down the moon'.

It seems that Glastonbury, by being a domain of the Goddess, was always linked to the Cauldron. In the thirteenth

---

[86] In a similar tale the nine Greek Muses gave inspiration to humans. The Grail Maidens are Bebhionn, Becuma, Almha, Blodeuwedd, Arduina, Beltane, Aeval, Nimmue and Water Faery.

[87] Alan Richardson, *The Magical Life of Dion Fortune* (Wellingborough: The Aquarian Press, 1991), p.180

century began its more celebrated association with the Holy Grail. That the Grail was originally a pagan symbol which transmuted into a Christian icon seems without doubt. It seems impossible to regard the cauldron as being the same physical size as the Grail, the advent of Christianity seems to make the latter shrink. Conversely, the spiritual heritage of the Grail has only increased.

The Grail has, at different times, been regarded as many different things. A horn of plenty for the questing knights, the two cruets of Joseph of Arimathea (one containing the blood, the other the sweat of Christ), the severed head of John the Baptist, the Dish of the Last Supper and a chalice filled with the Saviour's blood. Its appearance too seems to change. In Wolfram Von Eschenbach's *Parzival*, the Grail is portrayed as lying on green and gold *achmardi*—brocaded silk. As well as being the colour of the land[88] and thus life, it is significant that in ecclesiastical symbolism green is the colour of the Holy Ghost. To the mystics it is the colour of divinity. The Grail apparently also 'radiates a wonderful melody and a heavenly perfume'.[89]

As to the whereabouts of an actual artefact, as early as 1101 the *Sacro Catino*, the plunder of a Genoese campaign, was referred to as the 'Saint Grail'. Even earlier, Aldhelm, a scholar who later became Abbot of Malmesbury, may have introduced his monarch, Ina, the Christian king of Wessex (688-728), to a document entitled *The Holy Grail, Book I*, writings which implied the Grail was located in the Isle of Avalon. Other legends have cited Wearyall Hill,[90] Chalice Hill, and the Abbey in Glastonbury as possible locations where the Grail might be found.

---

[88] The successful discovery of the Grail restores fertility to the Waste Land and cures the wounded Fisher King.

[89] Jung, Franz, p. 297

[90] The Eastern slopes being known Fisher's Hill, an obvious reference to the Fisher King and Castle Carbonek.

In 1885, a Dr. Goodchild purchased a blue glass bowl in Bordighera, Italy, its silver leaf pattern interlaced with blue, green and amber floral designs. In 1898, apparently prompted by inner voices, Goodchild buried the bowl by the sluice at Beckery. In 1906 Wellesley Tudor-Pole, accompanied by Janet and Christine Allen, found the bowl. Tudor-Pole's daughter Katherine took it to her house in Royal York Crescent in Clifton, Bristol. She conducted ceremonies there which may have involved paeans of praise to Bride.

That the Grail is a female symbol is almost too obvious to mention. The Yoni, the *Vesica Piscis*—the power of female sexual energy was acknowledged and utilised by the Ancients. As Andrew Collins states,

> Once, chosen women, priestesses, would sit at the *dead centre* of their realms on stone 'thrones' and channel this divine light outwards to bring fecundity to the land, as well as divine revelation in the individual and contact with the One, the All. The *sri ma*, 'divine mothers', of India, still bear some knowledge of channeling this divine light, even today.[91]

Of the four elements, the chalice symbolises Water and the West. It is the cup of plenty, mercy and love, the womb, the cave. Descriptions of the Grail invariably mention its enchanting scents and sounds. The Grail is a sensual object. Knowing this, the Catholic Church introduced such an ambiance into the ceremony of Eucharist. As Terry Eagleton remarks 'Catholicism combined rigorous thought with sensuous symbolism.'[92]

Malory's fifteenth century *Morte d'Arthur* paves the way for the Holy Vessel, as a specifically Christian symbol, to be inaugurated into subsequent Grail literature. For later writers it

---

[91] Collins, p. 219

[92] Eagleton, *Observer* Review

becomes an amalgam of cultures—Celtic legend, Islamic love poetry and the Qabalah. As Malcolm Godwin informs us,

> The grail cannot really be separated from the undertaking of the quest for it. Both Grail and quest, the goal and the process towards that goal, embody the human fulfillment, whatever form the author wishes it to take.[93]

The scene against which the Grail is depicted changes as society does, but it seems to sit most comfortably in the Middle Ages. Why is this? Perhaps because the nobility of the knight seeks its complement in the divine beauty of woman. The king, and his relationship with the kingdom, is a theme beginning in the first age of kings, an era that possessed elements of the preceding matriarchal age. These are both sidereal periods of time, each consisting of two millennia and said to be ruled by an astrological sign. The age of kings is ruled by the cardinal fire sign, Aries, ruled by Mars. The matriarchal age is ruled by the fixed earth sign of Taurus, appointed to Venus.

By the end of the first millennium after Christ, His teachings had been distorted by an all-powerful Church as to be almost unrecognizable. The refusal by the established Church to acknowledge the Grail, despite it being embraced by Christians, is in accord with its paradoxical nature. The Grail, an obviously potent symbol, echoes the view of Ezra Pound on its *worth* to the individual:

> ...a symbol appearing in a vision has a certain richness and power of energizing joy—whereas if the supposed meaning of the symbol is familiar it has no

---

[93] Godwin, p. 14

more force, or interest of power of suggestion than any other word...[94]

The Grail can mean many different things to many different people, but always its purpose is *to enlighten*. Rudolf Steiner emphasises its power to fuel the imagination, as it is

> ...a free creation of the human spirit, that never would exist at all if we did not generate it ourselves. The task of understanding is not to replicate in conceptual form something that already exists, but rather to create a wholly new realm...[95]

Thus the Pagan regards the Cup very differently from the Christian, who sees it exclusively as a vehicle of redemption and salvation. Yet a third interpretation is *alchemical*, the Grail being seen as a means of rebirth or transformation. Its power can be ruthlessly destructive, as was demonstrated when the Grail was transmuted into the Ark of the Covenant and taken into battle by the Hebrews. As the Cauldron eschewed cowardice, so the Grail is no friend of the unworthy, and has the ability to expose artifice and strip away falsehood. In its metaphysical form the Grail releases a magical current, like waiting for a storm to blow itself out. Certainly the Grail 'is dangerous and harms those who are not aware that they should keep the distance enjoined.'[96]

---

[94] Ezra Pound, *Ezra Pound and Dorothy Shakespeare: Their Letters* (New Directions, 1993), p. 302

[95] Johannes Hemleben, *Rudolf Steiner: A Documentary Biography* (London: Henry Goulden, 1975), p. 37

[96] Jung, Franz, p. 389

New Age Mecca

Hark, hark the dogs do bark
The beggars are coming to town
Some in rags, some in tags
And one in a velvet gown.

Traditional Rhyme

In the 1950s probably the most exciting event that occurred in the small market town of Glastonbury was the annual cricket festival. Mervyn Kitchen and Roy Virgin would open the batting —Somerset C.C. at their finest, until the era of Richards and Botham. In the late Sixties the appearance of 'flower people' in Glastonbury was an inevitable accompaniment to the burgeoning spiritual search that took in sacred places. In those days you could climb the Tor and be almost certain to find yourself totally alone.

Geoffrey Ashe accurately predicted a sea change when in 1968 he wrote,

> Enthusiasts have predicted that Glastonbury's future, in some way which cannot yet be foreseen, will be greater than its past... many who have taken part in Glastonbury's renewal find themselves exploring the mystery by other paths.[97]

The catalyst was 'The Festival' in 1971. Things would never be the same again. In the 1980s many decided to leave the city and move to Glastonbury or the surrounding area, and even more came to visit or set up camp. It did not take long for

---

[97] Geoffrey Ashe, *The Quest for Arthur's Britain* (London: Granada Publishing, 1968) p. 125

Glastonbury, like Stonehenge, to become synonymous with *The New Age*. The term cannot be easily defined, though it appears that The New Age embraces every belief and creed and even invents a few new ones itself. It is most certainly not a 'world religion' in the traditional sense, yet its basic adherence to a form of spiritual mysticism seems to be its hallmark. As Marion Zimmer Bradley once wrote,

> Patterns alter and reform the evolution of the spirit which transcends immortality. Dreams survive for they are immortal and though the world should change entirely... that light shall not be lost to mankind so long as mankind still seeks solace in this holy earth called Avalon.[98]

The championing of 'spirit' or the 'universal force' reflects what are regarded as Aquarian values. The assumption that there is an 'interconnectedness of everything' is simply a holographic approach to the universe. Respect for the individual and the sanctity of particular places is emphasized, a perfectly sound philosophy, but not one that is particularly original.

In the twenty-first century, the High Street traders in Glastonbury openly refer to 'the season'. One would have to be extraordinarily naïve not to admit that Glastonbury, like nearby Cheddar or Wells, is yet another halt on the tourist circuit. Inevitably the town has changed and not always for the better. Talk of 'negative energies' is often rife, and when there are one too many raving drunks outside St. John's Church in the High Street, one might be forced to agree. Certainly many come to Glastonbury with high expectations and are just as deeply disappointed. Avalon does not reveal its secrets that easily. Silent contemplation, away from the crowd, in holy places—there may be found the key that unlocks the secret garden. If one comes seeking enlightenment it can be found; if one comes seeking bliss

---

[98] Marion Zimmer Bradley, *Lady of Avalon* (London: Viking Penguin, 1997)

that too is here. John Cowper Powys once described the cyclic nature of change in Glastonbury:

> Everyone who came to this spot seemed to draw something from it, attracted by a magnetism too powerful for anyone to resist, but as different people approached it they changed its chemistry, though not by essence, by their own identity, so that upon none of them it had the same psychic effect.[99]

West is the direction assigned to the element of Water and transcendence; and in the West of England lies Glastonbury, spiritual centre of Albion. At the most westerly point of the Isle of Avalon is Bride's Mound, forever to be associated with the Goddess. Those who come here feel her invisible presence as intensely as they experience the silver mist that caresses the moors. The Goddess has always been there in Britain. In past times she might have been ignored, suppressed, even ridiculed, but her influence has never entirely disappeared.

Bride's Mound is a place of transition—it lies between two worlds—timeless and yet vibrantly in the present. Here one can feel the spirits of those who went before, the Priest and Priestess of long ago who crossed the Great Water and entered the Inner Kingdom. Bride's Mound is the 'gateway to Avalon', and we who long ago discovered this, know it is a gift from the Queen of Heaven.

---

[99] Powys, p.1115

Bibliography

Agrippa, Cornelius, *Three Books of Occult Philosophy* (St Paul, MN: Llewellyn Publications, 1997)

Apuleius, Lucius *The Golden Ass*, Trans. P. G. Walsh (Oxford World's Classics)

Ashcroft-Nowicki, Dolores, *The Ritual Magic Workbook — A Practical Course of Self-Initiation* (Wellingborough: The Aquarian Press, 1986)

Ashe, Geoffrey, *The Quest for Arthur's Britain* (London: Granada Publishing, 1968)

Blavatsky, H. P. *The Secret Doctrine* (London: Theosophical Society, 1888)

Bligh-Bond, Frederick, *Hill of Vision—A Forecast of the Great War and the Social Revolution with the Coming of the New Race* (1919)

Bligh-Bond, Frederick *The Glastonbury Scripts Nos. 6 & 8* (London: The Scriptorium Publishing Association, 1924)

Bradley, Marion Zimmer, 'Thoughts on Avalon', *The Literary Womens' Trust*.

Bradley, Marion Zimmer *Lady of Avalon* (London: Viking Penguin, 1997)

Collins, Andrew *Twenty-First Century Grail—The Quest for a Legend* (London: Virgin Books, 2004)

Collins, Andrew *The Cygnus Mystery* (London: Watkins, 2006)

Cowper Powys, John *A Glastonbury Romance* (London: The Bodley Head, 1933)

Crowley, Aleister *The Confessions—An Autohagiography* (London: Arkana, 1989)

Demetra, George, *Mysteries of the Dark Moon* (San Francisco: Harper, 1992)

Eitel, Rev. E. J., *Handbook of Chinese Buddhism* (Hong Kong, 1873

Fortune, Dion, Aspects *of Occultism* (Wellingborough: The Aquarian Press, 1962)

Fortune, Dion, *Avalon of the Heart* (Wellingborough: The Aquarian Press, 1978)

Fortune, Dion, *Applied Magic and Aspects of Occultism* (London: Harper Collins, 1987)

Fortune, Dion, *The Training and Work of an Initiate* (London: The Aquarian Press, 1955)

Fortune, Dion, *The Sea Priestess* (New York: Samuel Weiser, 1999)

Fortune, Dion, *The Arthurian Formula* (Loughborough: Thoth Publications, 2006)

Gibbon, Monk, *The Masterpiece and the Man — Yeats as I Knew Him* (London: Rupert Hart-Davis, 1959)

Godwin, Malcolm, *The Holy Grail Its Origins, Secrets & Meaning Revealed* (London: Bloomsbury, 1994)

Hall, Manly P., *Secret Teaching of All Ages* (London: Penguin, 2003)

Hartley, Christine, *The Western Mystery Tradition — The Esoteric Heritage of the West* (Wellingborough: The Aquarian Press, 1968)

Hemleben, Johannes, *Rudolf Steiner: A Documentary Biography* (London: Henry Goulden, 1975)

Jelley, Harry, *Saint Patrick's Somerset Birthplace* (Somerset: Cary Valley Historical Publications, 1998)

Jung, C. G., *The Archetypes and the Collective Unconscious* (1926)

Jung, Emma and Von Franz, Marie-Louise, *The Grail Legend* (Princeton: Princeton University Press, 1998)

Kennish, Anthony John, *The Glastonbury Chronicles*

Knight, Gareth, *Dion Fortune and the Inner Light* (Loughborough: Thoth Publications, 2000)

Knight, Gareth, *Address at Leaping Hare Annual Conference* (April 1st 2006)

Lonegren, Sig, *Labyrinths, Ancient Myths and Modern Uses* (Glastonbury: Gothic Image, 1991)

Lumley Brown, Margaret, *The Arthurian Formula* Ed. Gareth Knight (London: Thoth Publications, 2006)

Malory, Sir Thomas, *Le Morte D'Arthur*, Ed. A. W. Pollard (London: Medici Society, 1929)

Maltwood, Katherine, *Enchantments of Britain* (London: James Clarke, 1982)

Maltwood, Katherine, *Glastonbury's Temple of the Stars* (London: James Clarke, 1982)

Mann, Nicholas *The Isle of Avalon- Sacred Mysteries of Arthur and Glastonbury* (London: Green Magic, 1996)

Mathers, Moina (High Priestess Anari), 'Isis Worship in France' (Article, 1899)

McMillan, Atasha 'Magical Mystery Tor', *Avalon Magazine* 20 (2002)

Merejkowski, Dimitri, *The Forerunner-The Romance of Leonardo da Vinci* (London: Constable and Company, 1933)

Michell, John, *New Light on the Ancient Mystery of Glastonbury* (Glastonbury: Gothic Image Publications, 1997)

Rahtz, Philip and Watts, Lorna, *Glastonbury Myth and Archaeology* (Gloucestershire: Tempus, 2003)

Richardson, Alan, *Priestess — The Life and Magic of Dion Fortune* (Loughborough: Thoth Publications, 2007)

Robertson, Olivia, *Nuit of the Milky Way* (London: F.O.I., 2007)

Royce, Alan, 'A Temple on the Tor', *Avalon Magazine* 21, (2002)

Sharp, Mrs. William (Arranger), *The Divine Adventure — The Works of "Fiona MacLeod", Vol. IV — Iona* (London: William Heinemann, 1925)

Stevens, Jose & Lena S., *Secrets of Shamanism* (New York: Avon Books, 2004)

Tennyson, Alfred Lord *'Morte D'Arthur', English Poetry III; From Tennyson to Whitman* (Boston USA: Harvard Classics)

Trevelyan, Sir George, *A Vision of the Aquarian Age* (London: Coventure Ltd, 1979)

Appendices

I

At The Well
The Rune of the Water Bearer

Ye have supped from the Pools of Sorrow,
Ye shall drink from the Wells of Joy!
The Golden Wheel is turning,
The heavenly spheres employ.
And she who bears the Measure
Shall stand in the dawn of day,
Pouring the waters of comfort
To the weary on the way.
Haste, O bride and bridegroom,
Behold the promised sign!
The hand that draws the Water
Has filled the cup with Wine!

Alice Buckton
1918

Bridie come in ~ your bed is ready
Traditional call

Your bed of straw and buttercups and daises,
your bed of swan-down and seashells,
you may rest in the meadows,
you may bathe in the pools,
you may rise in the mornings and walk the lands
from coast to coast
from valley to mountain
This is your land,
This is our home.

Bright Goddess Bridget
Imbolc Evocation

Bright Goddess Bridget,
Bringer of Light,
The Muse whose Poetry sings the world to life.
I call upon You as Goddess of Poetry and Guardian of the mirror
That brings true sight.
To help us all to see the power of words
To heal and bring light,
To all people and all countries torn apart by strife.

Bright Goddess Bridget,
Bringer of Light,
Keeper of the Eternal Sacred Flame.
I call upon You as Goddess of Smithcraft and the Hearth fire,
To rekindle the Divine Spark
Within our hearts once again.
So recognition of this within each one of us
Will engender love and peace to reign.

Bright Goddess Bridget,
Bringer of light.
I call upon you as the Goddess of the Healing at the Sacred Well
To cast upon us Your Magical Spell.
As you weave Your web of Alchemy
Transmuting dying winter's lethargy,
As you spread your green mantle o'er the Earth.
May Your Healing waters and Fiery Flame
Bring all that is good and healing to birth.

Jane Marshall
2003

Veil of Isis of Avalon

Look closely through the mists and you may see
A shadowy barge, gliding through the mists, once the Summer Sea
Evoking deep longings of coming home and forgotten soul memories
of the portal where souls enter the world and return to the stars.
For the sight of the Tor evokes memories of
                              the primal mound and calls our souls from afar
To this natural Temple of 'holiest erthe' and
                              running waters; lit by Sun, Moon and Stars.
Bird song forms symphony from Nature's band
as swans fly overhead and herons stand
like ghostly sentinels as creeping mist cloaks the land
forming the Veil of Isis in the Vale of Avalon.

Jane Marshall
2001

II

Starry Night Meditation

Relax. Deepen breathing to your rhythm. Visualise being in the Chalice Well gardens on a dark night, as the indigo canopy of the temple of stars spins above, and the stability of the earth beneath your feet supports you. Visualise walking through the peaceful, healing gardens until you reach the well-head and sit down. Focus on the third eye—your eye of vision. Feel your inner perception expand in this place of deep natural magic, where earth and water meet. Feel the aura of this peaceful, healing place envelop you.

Pause to reflect upon any unresolved emotional issues in your life—grief, loss being taken for granted, feeling unfulfilled, whatever is bothering you at this time. If you feel sad and lonely for a person or an animal or situation that has gone from your life, know that endings lead to new things just as day follows night, and that all things pass. If feelings or anxiety threaten to overwhelm you, remember that these are like tethers that keep us from moving for we are like the water of the red Spring, flowing towards earth as fear gradually moves us on to find our own level.

However, sometimes it is necessary to be still and wait rest and withdraw, in order to gather our energy into a still pool to replenish ourselves. At these times, nurture whatever bring peace—art, music, poetry, walking in Nature, meditation, whatever feels right, in order to plumb your hidden depths. Know that the well cannot be changed but constantly flows as we should, in harmony with the tides.

Know that our inner voice will only be heard when our still pool within is calm and unruffled by unruly thoughts and turbulent emotions, not necessarily our own. If troubled, we must not look frantically outside ourselves for advice and diversions, but look within for the answers to our problems. Remember that silence nourishes our spirits. Realise that we are never alone for the light from the heavenly realms and the inner light within us is shared by all of us, so in dark times, look to the light that links us all.

In your mind ask Isis to join you to your guiding star and sense an invisible thread of light pulling you up and its invisible radiance pouring into you. What do you sense, feel or know? Pause for a few minutes.

This reflected star mirrors our divine spark, so think of the six pointed star, symbol of balance and the seven rays of rainbow light of the garment of Isis of which we are all part. It is formed by the colours of the dancing stars and the planets, forming the Music of the Spheres, in the celestial current that moves the Boat of Millions of Years and the Barge of Avalon.

Feel the energy of earth and water rising up through your feet and the airy sparkling starry energy coming down through your crown to meet in your heart chakra. Feel love and healing peace in your heart as you ponder upon these words of Ancient Egyptian Wisdom:

> Heaven Above, Heaven Beneath,
> Starres Above, Starres beneath.,
> All this is Bellow is also Beneath,
> Understand this and be Happy.

Think how we as individuals could help to make the world a better place if we all acted from our hearts, from out true desire and not petty whims, rather than our heads. The heart centre is related to the Sun and the Spiritual Sun or Soul of the Sun, thought to be Sirius, Star of Isis, related to Venus, the green planet, the evening Star, the ruler of beauty and all life.

Remember, in the days to come, the balance of the six-pointed star, and if you hunch up, remember the invisible thread linking you to the your guiding star. Think also of the flowing well waters, the alchemical mix of the Red and White Springs and of the need to flow.

As you leave this scared place, think on this verse, which is the aim of any spiritual path.

> To see the world in Grain of sand,
> And heaven in a Wild flower
> Hold infinity in the palm of your hand
> And eternity in an hour.

Visualise walking down the path knowing that Winged Isis is rising as the Aquarian Phoenix from our unconscious minds. Her light unites us all, for she rises within me, within you, within the world, and as she rises so does Osiris.

Return to your time and place.

www.ingramcontent.com/pod-product-compliance
Lightning Source LLC
Chambersburg PA
CBHW071418040426
42445CB00012BA/1196